WOW!

Wonders of Water

Girl Scouts of the USA

**Chair, National
Board of Directors**

**Kathy Hopinkah
Hannan**

**Chief
Executive Officer**

Sylvia Acevedo

**Vice President,
Girl Experience**

Jennifer Allebach

girl scouts

Photographs

Page 25: NASA/courtesy of
nasaimages.org;
Page 28: by Mike Murphy;
Pages 49, 51: courtesy of
Water for People;
Page 71: courtesy
of Miwa Koizumi;
Page 82: ©E. Widder;
Page 86: courtesy of Blue
Legacy International;
Page 104: courtesy of
Pelamis Wave Power

The women mentioned in
this book are examples of
how women have used their
voice in the world. This
doesn't mean that GSUSA
(or you) will agree with
everything they have ever
done or said.

SENIOR DIRECTOR, PROGRAM RESOURCES:
Suzanne Harper

ART DIRECTOR: Douglas Bantz

WRITERS: Anne Marie Welsh & Leigh Fenly

CONTRIBUTORS: Amélie Cherlin, Rochana
Rapkins, María Caban, Kathleen Sweeney, Carol
Fleishman

ILLUSTRATOR: Helena Garcia

DESIGNER: Alexander Isley Inc.

EXECUTIVE EDITOR, JOURNEYS: Laura Tuchman

MANAGER, OPERATIONS: Sharon Kaplan

MANAGER, PROGRAM DESIGN: Sarah Micklem

First published in 2009 by Girl Scouts of the USA
420 Fifth Avenue, New York, NY 10018-2798

www.girlscouts.org

ISBN: 978-0-88441-732-3

Printed in Italy

14 15/19 18 17

What's in WOW!

Welcome to WOW

SLIDE SPRINKLE SPRAY DIP

WOW! Water gives you so many ways to get wet and have fun. Stand in the rain. Jump in a lake. Feel the fog. Glide on ice.

Look around and think of all the places you might find water indoors and out.

Life can't exist without water. Neither can rainbows!

Brownie friends Alejandra, Campbell, and Jamila are starting a journey about all the Wonders of Water! And so are you! As you travel, you will see that WOW doesn't just mean Wonders of Water. For Girl Scout Brownies, it also means Ways of Working.

WOW!

SHOWER   **DIVE**

SWIM   **SPLASH**

You'll WOW yourself and everybody else as you wind your way through this WOW journey. How? By being just like water!

You'll begin by loving water drop by drop. Your drops will join with your Brownie friends' drops to form a stream of water. As you love and save water together, that stream will move forward like a mighty river. As you reach out and share your water-loving ways, that river will flow into an ocean.

LOVE water, SAVE water, SHARE water.

Now, that's a very big WOW!

One Sparkly Drop

School was out and it was a rainy afternoon. Jamila, Alejandra, and Campbell walked home, splashing in every puddle.

"Where does water go after the rain stops?" asked Alejandra. "Some runs down the street. But where does the rest go?"

"I think it just disappears," Campbell said.

"Hey, look! We can see ourselves in this puddle," Jamila called out. "Come closer."

The three girls huddled by the puddle.

WORDS WORTH KNOWING

When something is REFLECTED, you see its image bouncing off a smooth surface.

Alejandra loves to splash in the rain.

Campbell loves to swim in the lake.

Jamila loves to walk in the fog.

"I know who we can ask," Alejandra said, jiggling the charm on her bracelet. They looked at their faces reflected in the water. Then each girl held out her arm and wiggled her charm.

"Twist me and turn me and show me the elf. I looked in the water and saw my . . . self." The girls chanted the words together, slowly.

Suddenly a fourth face stared back at them from the puddle.

"You called?" asked Brownie Elf.

"We did," said Jamila, smiling down at their small friend.

What do you like to do with water?

_____

_____

_____

_____

"We want to know what happens to water after it rains," said Campbell.

"That's easy," said the elf. "Water is moving and changing all the time. Let's follow a sparkly drop."

She scooped up a handful of water and threw it in the air. The girls looked up. A rainbow appeared.

Then a giant bubble floated down around them and lifted them up. The girls could now see the water drop up close.

"I can see its tiny sparkle!" Campbell shouted. The drop rose and became misty. It joined other drops and turned bright violet in the rainbow.

WORDS
WORTH
KNOWING | VAPOR means
moisture in the air,
like fog, mist, or steam.

"The color of my raincoat!" Jamila exclaimed.
The girls stared and smiled. The yellow of
Alejandra's slicker and the red of Campbell's coat
were also in the rainbow.

"The rainwater in the puddle only seemed to
disappear," Brownie Elf said. "It became **vapor**."

"Is that what happens to my dog Tango's
water when his bowl sits in the sun all day?"
Campbell asked.

"Or what happens to water in a saucepan
when we boil eggs for too long?" asked Alejandra.

"That's right," said Brownie Elf.

Rainbows

A big and beautiful WOW!

Have you ever wondered how rainbows are made? Lots of water droplets float in the air during and right after a rain. When sunlight hits them, it bends. This bending separates the light into bands of color—red, orange, yellow, green, blue, indigo, and violet. Then the colors are reflected back through the water droplets for you to see. A rainbow's colors are all the colors found in sunlight. That's why you see a big, beautiful, multicolored arc of light after a rain.

But you won't see a rainbow after every rain. Rainbows need bright sun and rain at the same time. They also need the sun to come from one direction and the rain to come from the opposite direction. The brightest rainbows appear when the sun is low in the sky behind you and a heavy rain is in front of you.

Name the rainbow's colors!
(Hint: Think ROY G. BIV!)

Red
Orenge
yellow
Green
Blue
indogo
viloet

"And when sunlight shines on lots of misty water in the right way, you see a rainbow," the elf added. The girls watched the rainbow fade and the sparkle rise higher. It became a water drop again, this time part of a fluffy cloud.

"That's what clouds are made of: misty vapor turned back into water drops. I'll show you more of that later," Brownie Elf promised.

"I've seen droplets dribble down the window when I take a hot shower," said Jamila.

"Same thing," said Brownie Elf. "That change is called condensation."

The sparkly water drop rose higher.

Then it froze.

"Now it looks like **crystal**," Alejandra exclaimed.

Flying Saucers?

The biggest snowflake in the world fell in Montana in 1887. It was 15 inches across. Another big flake fell in Siberia in 1971. It was 12 inches by 8 inches. Do you know where Siberia is?

"It's a snowflake," Campbell said. "Wow!"

The girls watched the snowflake dart and dance. The wind blew it here and there. Then it flew right by them. Down and down it went. Down and down the girls followed. The air became warmer. A strong wind blew the snowflake away.

"It's melting into water," Campbell said.

"Awesome!" said Jamila. "Look how far it's gone."

"And how many things it's been!" said Alejandra.

"I wonder what it will do next," Campbell said as she ran ahead.

Brownies of long ago and today!

The first Brownie "pack" in the United States started in Massachusetts in 1916. That was probably when your mother's grandmother—your great-grandmother—was a little girl.

Girl Scouts have had a Promise and a Law for a long time. You can read them both on the inside cover of this book. Take a look at the Girl Scout Law. Which lines do you think match what the Brownie friends are learning in this story?

WORDS
WORTH
KNOWING

GROUNDWATER
is water beneath Earth's
surface in open spaces or
cracks in rocks. It can
flow upward as a spring
or even as a desert oasis.

"Will it ever stop changing?" Jamila asked.

Brownie Elf smiled. "Water's journey never really ends. It's a circle that keeps going around, like bicycle wheels. No beginning and no end. That's why it's called the water *cycle*."

"Hmm," said Campbell. "So we can't follow it to the end—because there is no end! But maybe a little longer? Please?"

In a forest clearing, the sparkly drop landed at the foot of a tree. Then it vanished.

"Did it go underground?" Campbell asked.

"Yes," said Brownie Elf. "And it may be moving deeper down as **groundwater**."

"What's that?" Alejandra asked.

"Well," answered Brownie Elf, "under the ground, water gets stored in many places. Sometimes it bubbles up in springs."

The four walked toward a small stream.

"Go ahead and feel it," Brownie Elf suggested.

"Yikes!" Jamila shouted. "It's cold."

"Yes, it's cold, but it's also very clean. There's our sparkly drop again," Brownie Elf said, pointing to a glimmer on the surface of the water.

The Water Cycle

The amount of water on Earth is always the same, but it is constantly moving from the oceans to the air to the land and back again.

CONDENSATION

The vapor turns into a cloud, which is a group of teeny-tiny water droplets. The wind carries the cloud over to the land.

PRECIPITATION

As the air cools, the teeny-tiny droplets get bigger and heavier and fall to Earth in the form of rain, snow, sleet, or hail.

RUNOFF

The water that falls on the land goes into the rivers and lakes and then flows back into the oceans.

EVAPORATION

The sun shines over the ocean and heats the water, which becomes a vapor.

S.S. BROWNIE

Be Prepared for Wonders of Water!

Early Brownies used the same Girl Scout motto as you:
Be Prepared! And they had a slogan, too: Do a Good Turn Daily!
Being prepared and doing a good turn daily will serve you well
on this Wonders of Water Journey! What other slogan might you
like to use? Write it here:

_____

_____

"How'd it get there?" asked Campbell. "And
so fast?"

"Sometimes I can speed up time," the elf said
with a wink. "The drop raced underground over
rocks and stones. Then it came out fresh and clean
in a spring. The spring fed this small stream and
now it's joining a bigger stream called a river."

The drop was already rising again from
the water's surface.

"I get it," Alejandra said. "The drop is starting
its journey all over again."

When the drop joined a cloud growing heavier
and darker, they heard a BOOM! At the first clap
of thunder, Brownie Elf led the girls to the safety
of a porch. From there they watched the storm.

WORDS
WORTH
KNOWING

TRICKLING is a
small flow of liquid that
may sound all tinkly to
your ears, like a stream
flowing over rocks or rain
running along a curb.

This time the drop fell as rain and landed on a rooftop. It dripped past the girls' noses, splashed on the sidewalk, and rolled toward the street.

Truck exhaust mixed with the **trickling** rainwater. So did plastic bottles and old candy wrappers. The water drop's sparkle faded.

"All that junk is making the water dirty," Campbell said. "And look, there's oily stuff in it, too."

"The water is heading to a drain," Jamila said.

Water Wisdom

You notice the bathroom faucet is dripping. What should you do?

A. Put a pan under the faucet and use the water to fill your dog's bowl.

B. Observe the drops. If there aren't that many, don't worry about it.

C. Tell your parents so they can get it fixed and do A until then.

Answer: C—Even small drops add up. Thirty drops a minute can add up to more than two gallons of water wasted each day. Leaks are some of the biggest water wasters at home.

"When water races over the ground like this, it's called runoff. And that's a storm drain," Brownie Elf said.

"Dirty air and litter made the sparkly drop look so sad," Alejandra said. "Can it ever get clean again?"

"Some water drops do," the elf said. "But dirty water can be very hard for people to clean. It's best to keep it pure from the start; the whole world shares the same water."

"So if we make the water dirty, we might be taking clean water away from people living somewhere else?" Alejandra asked.

"That's right, Ali," said Brownie Elf.

The girls and the elf walked to the sea. A pipe carrying storm runoff was jutting over the water.

Brownie Elf soon spotted the drop they had been following as it made its way out of the pipe and into the sea.

"Maybe it will go to Mexico," Campbell said.

"Maybe it will come out of the faucet in my kitchen and I'll drink it!" said Alejandra.

"Maybe it will be blown on a cloud to China, then rain down into a river," Jamila said.

Water Wisdom

It's so hot outside you could probably fry an egg on the sidewalk. What's the best way to cool off outdoors?

A. Turn on the lawn sprinklers for 30 minutes.

B. Fill up all your water toys—soakers and spray bottles—and invite your friends over.

C. Fill a wading pool and jump in with your friends.

Answer: B—Thirty minutes of sprinkling uses 70 gallons of water. Even a small wading pool takes 100 gallons to fill. But you could get your friends soaked to the skin with soakers for less than 10 gallons.

Time for a WOW!

Good Friends Stick Together

What do you notice about Jamila, Campbell, and Alejandra that shows they are good friends?

_____

What do you notice about how they are alike and how they are different?

_____

What do you do to show you are a good friend?

_____

How are you like your friends? How are you different?

_____

"And then rush over a mountain as a waterfall," Brownie Elf added.

"Lucky drop. I would love to go to China," said Jamila. "But we should probably go home now."

"Yes, let's get you home," said Brownie Elf.

And—*poof*—they were back at their rain puddle.

"When you're ready for a new adventure, you know how to find me!" the elf told the girls. "We'll visit wetlands and see wonderful water creatures."

"Thank you! Thank you!" the girls said. And with a *poof*, the elf was gone.

Water Wisdom

In your neighborhood, the sidewalks and driveways are getting dirty, so you tell everyone, "Bring out those hoses and give it a good cleaning." Is there a better way?

A. Yes, you can use a broom instead.

B. No, stick with the hose.

C. Use an electric power washer to blast that grime away.

Answer: A—Save water and get a little healthy workout by sweeping rather than washing.

Time for a WOW!

Teaching and Inspiring Others

When Brownie Elf shows the girls how water travels in a cycle, she is passing on her knowledge. And in doing so, she inspires the girls. Now they, too, want to help keep water clean.

What have you learned about loving water that you can teach others? What will you ask others to do to show that they love water?

_____

_____

"Water does so many amazing things," said Campbell. "I can't wait to see more."

"Me, too," said Alejandra. "I think we should promise to keep our water clean."

"And not waste water," said Jamila. "Water is one more thing everybody shares!"

And then the three girls formed a Brownie Good-bye Circle before heading home.

POOF!

The Blue Planet

Earth is called the Blue Planet. That's because so much of it is covered with water. From outer space, Earth looks mostly blue. That's all the liquid water. Earth has frozen water at the poles and in glaciers. From outer space, those places look white.

How much of Earth is water? Three out of four parts are covered with it. So if Earth were a dollar, three quarters of it would be water. That's a lot of blue!

But most of that water is in the oceans. We can't drink saltwater or use it to grow food or plants and flowers.

Just 3 percent of the water on Earth is fresh water. Think of it this way: If all the water on Earth equaled 100 drops, just three of those drops would be fresh enough to use.

A lot of the planet's water is locked in glaciers and polar ice caps. Of the rest, half is beneath the Earth's surface. Remember Brownie Elf and the groundwater?

With billions of people living on Earth, that's not a lot of water to drink and to use. That's why it's so important to save water and keep it clean.

WORDS WORTH KNOWING | Earth's **POLES** are the South Pole in Antarctica and the North Pole in the Arctic Ocean. Imagine Earth spinning like a top. The poles are the farthest ends and they are frozen solid.

GS

WORDS WORTH KNOWING | **GLACIERS** are huge sheets of ice formed when snow gathers and freezes. Thick, slow-moving glaciers often look soft blue.

A World That's Wet and Dry

Water is so important that some people created ceremonies to honor the rain. The Zuni of the American Southwest wore turquoise as a symbol of rain when they performed rain dances.

Arctic Ocean

In **SEATTLE**, Washington, barrels atop City Hall collect enough rain for the garden and to flush all the toilets.

ICELAND generates 80 percent of its electricity from waterpower.

Pacific Ocean

NORTH AMERICA

Atlantic Ocean

CAMELS can go more than a week without water. When they do drink, they can take in 32 gallons at one time. That's 512 8-ounce glasses!

AFRICA

MOUNT WAI'ALE'ALE on Kauai, Hawaii, gets more than 460 inches of rain every year. That's more than one inch a day!

The **AMAZON RIVER** has more water than the Nile, Mississippi, and Yangtze rivers combined.

SOUTH AMERICA

Annual Precipitation

Less than 10 inches
Less than 250 millimeters

10 to 20 inches
250 to 500 millimeters

20 to 40 inches
500 to 1,000 millimeters

40 to 80 inches
1,000 to 2,000 millimeters

80 to 120 inches
2,000 to 3,000 millimeters

More than 120 inches
More than 3,000 millimeters

Scientists tested water from **MARS** and said it was "very fine."

OUTER SPACE

EUROPE

ASIA

There are 45,000 dams in the world. Nearly half are in **CHINA**.

ELEPHANTS drink up to 50 gallons of water each day. That's 100 times the amount recommended to humans.

Farmers in **EGYPT** are lucky if rain falls a few days a year.

Indian Ocean

At about 80 million years old, the **INDIAN OCEAN** is the youngest ocean in the world.

KOALAS get their water by eating eucalyptus leaves. The name koala means "no drink."

AUSTRALIA

About 90 percent of the ice on Earth is in **ANTARCTICA.** Brrrr!

ANTARCTICA

WORDS WORTH KNOWING

A CEREMONY is something you do to celebrate a tradition. A ceremony connects you to others who share the same feelings.

A REAL RAIN CATCHER

Frances Lamberts bought a house in Jonesborough, Tennessee, 30 years ago. The house sat on an acre of land and had five trees. To attract birds, Frances planted more trees. She chose native trees that didn't need extra care.

She also planted gardens and fed them with rich soil called compost that she made from food scraps, leaves, and grass.

She collected rainwater in old honey barrels. And she created a pond to catch rain runoff from her roof. "I make use of all the rainwater I can collect," she says.

Her land is now home to more than 100 trees, and insects, birds, ducks, sheep, and all kinds of wildlife. The land, which includes an orchard, produces almost all of Frances's food. She only has to buy grains and dairy products.

Time for a WOW!

Loving Water

Frances Lamberts saves a lot of water. That's using resources wisely, just like the Girl Scout Law suggests. And that's loving water, too! Where in your life do you see water that needs better care?

Do you see . . .
good water poured down a drain when it could be used for something else, like watering plants? water faucets dripping all day?

My Ideas for Loving Water

_____

_____

_____

Encourage your family and friends to love water, too!

Remember: There are 800,000 Girl Scout Brownies and they all have families. Imagine how much water would be saved if each of you pitched in and inspired your schools and communities to pitch in, too!

Your Own Wonders of Water— WOW!

A Water Map and Water Journal in One!

Map your Wonders of Water! Write or draw or paste photos of all your water places. Record favorite water sightings—even rain, snow, or hail! What does your weather watching tell you about water?

As you get wise to the Wonders of Water, keep mapping! Add what you see, what you love, and what you wonder about. Do you love the sound of water flowing in a fountain? Do you wonder about a pond's gooey-looking water? Use your WOW map to list ways to save and protect water. Fill it with all your project ideas!

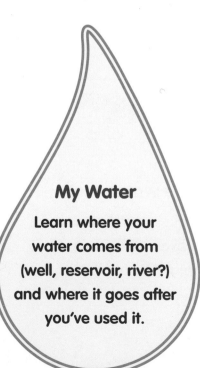

My Water

Learn where your water comes from (well, reservoir, river?) and where it goes after you've used it.

Part 2

A Ride Through the Wetlands

Are you ready?" Alejandra asked excitedly.

"I can't wait!" Campbell said.

Jamila jumped up and down. "Me neither!"

The three girls had spent the day together at Alejandra's *rancho*. They had ridden her pony, Ladybug, and had a picnic in the woods with her *abuelo*, who brought sandwiches called *tortas*.

He showed them pink flowers hiding under the leaves near where they had eaten. Then they each filled a canteen with cool water from the creek.

Now, in Alejandra's room, with their creek water mixed in a big blue bowl, the girls were ready. It had seemed like a lifetime since they'd floated in a bubble and seen a rainbow. They hadn't been able to think of anything else. Most of all, they remembered that Brownie Elf had promised them another water adventure. They were going to the wetlands. They were ready for it!

"I hope there aren't alligators in the wetlands," Campbell said in a hushed voice.

Time for a WOW!

Exploring People's Differences

Campbell laughed when she saw the *tortas* because she thought a *torta* would be a cake. She knew the English word "torte," which is a round cake. "Understanding differences among people is more important than the foods we eat or the words we use," Alejandra's *abuelo* said. "Differences are not something to poke fun at. They're something to honor and cherish. Our differences are what make the world so fascinating!"

When have you made fun of someone who was different from you?

_____

How do you think the person felt?

_____

When you see someone being made fun of, what will you do to stop it?

_____

"I think there will be pretty flowers, like at Ali's *rancho*," Jamila said to make her friend feel safer.

The three girls stared into the bowl of creek water and recited their rhyme. In a flash, Brownie Elf appeared. She had a dragonfly in one hand and a small green lizard in the other. "Hello, again," she called. "I've missed you!"

"We've missed you, too!" the girls said.

"I hope your arms are strong, because the best way to see a wetland is by kayak," Brownie Elf said. "That means you need to paddle."

"We can! We can!" the girls said.

Twist Me and Turn Me . . .

"Twist me and turn me and show me the elf.
I looked in the water and saw ___myself___."
Those words with the fill-in-the-blank at the end are part of the earliest Girl Scout Brownie story—and of every Brownie story since.

Alejandra, Campbell, and Jamila know the words by heart—even the missing one. That word, *myself*, was a signal for early Girl Scout Brownies. It let them know that they were capable of doing good things.

In the ELF Adventure, the girls say those words whenever they want to visit with Brownie Elf.

Brownies who are all grown up still remember those beloved lines. When you're older, you may find yourself remembering them, too!

"Then grab a life jacket and hop in."

The girls looked at one another quickly and then slipped into the kayak. The paddles were light in their hands.

Brownie Elf steered the kayak through a narrow passageway of dark blue water.

But it was hardly quiet. The dragonfly buzzed about their heads, birds cuck-cucked, bullfrogs bellowed, ducks quacked. The lizard darted about in the bottom of the kayak.

Around them, trees grew right down to the water, making it shady and cool. Gray moss, almost the color of *abuelo*'s beard, hung from the tree branches.

My Paddle

My paddle's keen
and bright
Flashing like silver
Follow the wild goose flight
Dip, dip, and swing

Dip, dip, and swing
her back
Flashing like silver
Follow the wild goose
track
Dip, dip, and swing

Margaret Embers
McGee, 1918

"This looks like a place out of dinosaur times," Jamila said softly.

"Wetlands have been around for a very long time," Brownie Elf said. "A hundred years ago, some people thought they were useless and even dangerous. People could drown in them, and there were mosquitoes and alligators and snakes. But that was before we learned how important wetlands and wetland creatures are."

S.S. BROWNIE

MAKING ROOM FOR PICKLE PLANTS

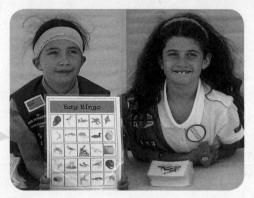

Sibyl Martinez is working to restore Bothin Marsh, a wetland in Mill Valley, California. Sibyl, 10, and her Brownie sister, **Milagros**, 8, live in Tiburon, not far from the marsh. Their troop and others nearby adopted the marsh as part of a larger Girl Scout effort called Save the Bay. Through Save the Bay, Girl Scouts all over the San Francisco Bay region are exploring local wetlands and educating and inspiring others to protect them.

The most important thing at Bothin Marsh is for the marsh's plants to have room to grow, because they provide food for all the marsh's creatures. "If native plants can't grow, then the native animals that eat those plants can't survive either," Sibyl explains.

Besides clearing out vegetation like broom and ice plant, which crowd out the marsh's food-giving plants, Sibyl teaches others about the plants and wildlife of the Bay Area. She uses a game called Bay Bingo, with cards that show 54 plants and animals, including the purple shore crab, a long-legged bird called an egret, and the Tiburon salmon.

Sibyl has seen good results in Bothin Marsh since she and her friends began working to protect it. "Now we're seeing pickleweed again," she says with a laugh. "It's a native plant that's green and looks like a pickle."

What wetlands are in your area? What's being done to protect them?

_____

WORDS
WORTH
KNOWING

EXTINCT
means something
no longer exists, like
dinosaurs. For animals,
extinction stinks!

"Why are they important?" Alejandra asked.

"I think I know one reason," Campbell said. "Look at all the animals and plants here. Wetlands must be a good home for them."

"You're right," Brownie Elf agreed. "Wetlands are home for lots of plants and animals, more than any other place on Earth. But the sad thing is that half of them are being harmed by changes in the environment. That means they might even become **extinct**."

The girls were quiet then, as each thought about what the world would be like without so many living things. The kayak glided along the shore past huge clumps of tall grasses.

"Do all wetlands look like this?" Jamila asked.

"Good question," Brownie Elf answered. "Wetlands can be really big, like this one, or so tiny that they're called 'prairie potholes.' They can be close to the ocean and full of saltwater plants and animals, or just a puddle in the middle of a meadow far from the sea."

"What's that?" Alejandra asked. There was a slapping sound in the water.

"A beaver!" Brownie Elf said as she edged the kayak closer. They all saw a large flat tail disappear into the water.

"We must have scared her," Brownie Elf said. "Beavers slap their tails on the water to warn other beavers when they sense danger. It's lucky we saw her. She's one of the reasons we can even be here."

"I know beavers build dams," Campbell said, "but why couldn't we be here without her?"

Brownie Elf took a deep breath. "Beavers like to build dams in low areas between hills where there is a stream. The area around their dams captures water and becomes a wetland. Once there's a wetland, all the creatures come to live in it—like the egrets you see in the water and hear in the trees, and the turtles and snakes and frogs.

Water Wisdom

You've been finger painting all afternoon.
You can't wait to get cleaned up. How should you do it?

A. Take a bath, but fill the tub just halfway. That's enough to get good and wet.

B. Take a bath and be sure to fill the tub to the brim. You need a lot of water to get rid of all that paint.

C. Take a shower. It uses the least amount of water and you won't be sitting in paint-filled water!

Answer: A or C—Filling a tub only halfway saves 25 gallons for every bath. Over a year, that's enough to fill 100,000 glasses of water. And a tub filled halfway is plenty of water for getting clean. But a short shower uses even less water.

"Do you remember how you saw the water running through the streets after the storm?" Brownie Elf asked. "And how dirty it was?"

The girls nodded.

"Well, a wetland is a place where water can get cleaned," she said. "The clean water can then be used by animals and humans. We all need clean water to live."

Jamila looked around at the ripples on the water sliding onto the shore, one after the other.

"Then this must be Earth's washing machine!" she said.

Brownie Elf chuckled. "I never thought of it that way, but you are exactly right!"

As the four headed back to Ali's *rancho*, Campbell began to look worried. "Now I understand why water is so important. But are there any places without water?"

"There are places with very little water," Brownie Elf answered. "One of them is a long, long way from here in South America, in the Atacama Desert. It's so dry there that in many parts no one has ever seen a drop of rain."

"That must be terrible," Alejandra said, thinking of how she loved rainstorms.

Water Wisdom

You wake up in the middle of the night and hear the sound of the toilet running. What should you do?

A. Go back to sleep and forget about it.

B. Next morning, tell your parents the toilet needs to be fixed.

C. Get out of bed and jiggle the handle.

Answer: C—A toilet that isn't working correctly can waste 25 gallons of water a day; that's enough to fill a bathtub halfway. Remember, too, that sometimes toilets have leaks that you can't hear. Here's an easy way to test your toilet: Ask an adult to lift the lid of the tank so you can add 10 drops of food coloring to the water. If the water in the toilet bowl changes color, you have a leak.

"But even though the desert is dry, it gets a lot of fog," Brownie Elf continued. "Some plants use that fog as food. And now, people in one village have figured out how to 'catch' the fog. They collect enough water for gardens and to take showers every day."

"So the people learned about water from the trees and plants!" Campbell said excitedly. "When fog turns into water, that change has a special name," she added with a grin. She exchanged a knowing look with Jamila and Alejandra.

"Condensation! Condensation!" the three girls chanted.

Loving the Great Outdoors!

The Brownie friends have promised to spend more time in nature, enjoying all its wonders. How about you and your friends?

What do you see when you are quiet in nature? What will you do to make good use of your Brownie energy when you're outdoors?

_____

_____

"It's time to say good-bye until next time," Brownie Elf said, guiding the kayak back to their starting point. She scooped up the dragonfly in one hand and the lizard in the other.

"You know how to find me when you're ready for another adventure."

The girls waved good-bye and then—*poof!*— Brownie Elf disappeared.

Just as suddenly, Alejandra, Jamila, and Campbell were back in Alejandra's room, pleasantly tired from their adventure.

"Let's make a promise," Alejandra said. "Every day, let's spend time outdoors just being quiet."

Campbell said, "If we're quiet, we might see lots of things—even lots of animals, like in the wetlands."

"If we look a lot," Jamila added, "we could learn a lot, just like the people in the desert. Maybe someday we could invent something to help the wetlands."

Then the girls formed a Brownie Good-bye Circle and made their promise to spend time enjoying the wonders of the great outdoors.

Your Water Body

Your body is constantly taking in and passing out water. It's a cycle, like the worldwide water cycle. You take in water when you drink it and when you eat foods that have water in them. Do you know how you flush water out of your body?

Your body is 65 percent water. Are you surprised?

How I Use Water

Write all the ways that you use water and how much you think you use. You might think of a gallon jug of water. How many jugs of water would your use of water fill?

_____

_____

_____

Figure out the amount of water in your body in pounds. Ask a friend or family member to help you:

Your weight in pounds x .65 = Your water weight

_____

Now imagine that you had to gather all that water on your own and carry it a long distance to your home.

How might you change your water-use habits? Look at your list of water uses and cross off any that you could do without!

Drink Up!

Water is important because it feeds your heart, brain, and muscles. How much water do you think you drink each day? Four or five eight-ounce glasses a day is a good amount to help you stay healthy. See if you can drink that much each day for a week. One of those glasses of water will probably come from the food you eat. Some foods—like watermelon (yum!) and tomatoes (one of Campbell's favorite foods)— are nearly all water. Other good choices are milk, herbal tea, and fruit and vegetable juices.

How We Use Water

People need at least five gallons of water a day, according to the World Health Organization. In the United States and Japan, each person uses, on average, 100 gallons of water a day. In parts of Africa, people get by with only two to three gallons a day.

Taking a bath = **36** gallons of water

Five-minute shower = **25** gallons

Hand-washing dishes = **20** gallons

Running the dishwasher = **15** gallons

Brushing your teeth = **2** gallons if you leave the tap running, ½ gallon if you turn it off

Flushing the toilet = **3** to **5** gallons

Running the washing machine = **40** gallons

What can you do?

• Put a jug of water inside the toilet tank; the toilet will use less water when you flush.

• Put a bucket in the shower and a bucket outside when it rains; use the water you collect to water plants.

Did you know?

We need water to grow everything we eat and to produce many things we use every day.

• It takes **45** gallons of water to make one glass of orange juice. That includes growing the oranges, of course.

• It takes **700** gallons of water to make a cotton T-shirt, including the water the cotton plants drink in order to grow!

A Wide World of Water Vessels

Not everyone in the world has water piped into their homes. Some people must find their own water. Sometimes that water comes from a stream or a spring, or it might be collected from a well. In countries with little rainfall, rainwater is collected in large bins and stored for later use.

Collecting and carrying water is done mostly by women and children. Children sometimes carry water in bags made of animal hide that they sling over their shoulders. Or they team up to collect water in a large metal tub.

Women may balance huge jars of water on their heads. They often carry more than their weight in water every day. Imagine carrying that much water every day! How would that feel?

No More Heavy Lifting

Just a few years ago in the remote Malkangiri district of India, women had to spend most of their time collecting water. Every day in summer, they carried pots and other vessels along hilly roads to the closest stream, which was miles away.

The women from the district's five villages decided they needed to make a change. More than 100 women began a project to cut, polish, and connect pipes made of bamboo, a strong plant that grows in their region, so that water could be piped from the stream to their villages.

When water began to flow to the villages, the women no longer had to spend their days carrying it. They had more time for other important things. Their teamwork now benefits 800 people!

BRINGING CLEAN WATER HOME

Elisa Speranza loves working with water. She grew up in Lynn, Massachusetts, where she was a Girl Scout and always cared about the environment. For her career, "I went where my passion took me," she says.

Elisa works at CH2M HILL, a company that helps cities all over the United States with many things, including water-treatment plants. She's also the former chair of the board of Water for People, a nonprofit created by water professionals to help other countries obtain clean drinking water.

Water for People "doesn't send volunteers to dig wells and trenches," Elisa says. "We make it possible for local people to build projects themselves." Those projects include building simple toilets and outdoor hand-washing stations.

Having clean water is important for everyone, but in many countries, it's especially important for girls. When clean water isn't easily available, girls must help get it, and that means they can't attend school.

"They are expected to help their mothers haul water from a well or stream. They may spend four or five hours a day hauling water," Elisa explains. When water can be piped to a village, the girls no longer have to haul it. That is a huge change in their lives.

Clean Water to Drink

More than one billion people in the world cannot count on having safe drinking water. That's about one-sixth of all the people on Earth.

How Do You Carry Water?

In 2007, people in the United States bought 22 billion plastic bottles of water. Can you imagine that many bottles piled in the garbage?

When you camp or hike, do you carry bottled water or do you use a canteen? Canteens and other containers that you can use again and again are better for the planet than plastic bottles of water. Why? Because plastic bottles are thrown away after one use and they often don't get recycled. Some end up floating in the ocean, where they harm sea life!

What could you and your Brownie group do to get people to stop buying bottled water? How could you get your school or your community to join your effort?

CLEANING WATER WITH LIGHT

Florence Cassassuce

grew up in France and has lived all over the world. She studied math and physics and became an environmental engineer. Her job lets her combine technology and nature, and help people.

A few years ago, Florence learned that thousands of people in Baja California Sur in Mexico were getting sick from dirty water. Chemicals from farms, waste from animals, and trash thrown in rivers had gotten into their well water.

Florence knew that a special kind of light called ultraviolet, or UV, light can make dirty water clean again. UV light kills bacteria and viruses that can make people sick. Florence and her team worked with people in Mexico to make large plastic buckets fitted with a UV lightbulb. Families pour well water into the buckets and then turn on the UV light. Soon the water is pure enough to drink. The buckets let hundreds of families have clean drinking water.

Florence continues to work on ways for people to have clean water. "Your heart drives you to come back and do more," she says.

What will you design?

Engineers like Florence invent things. They put technology to use to help people and the planet. What gadget would you create to help both people and water?

Time for a WOW!

Tips for Talking!

Now that you've started thinking about what you love about water and how we all need to treasure this precious resource, you can start inspiring others. These tips will come in handy when you want to talk to people about treating water well!

1. Be Kind!

You want people to be good to water. So try not to blame anyone for what they are doing right now. Instead of saying, "You're bad! You'd better turn off that faucet," offer some useful information. You could say, "Did you know that only 1 percent of water on the planet is drinkable? That's why it's important not to waste it."

What else might you say?

_____

_____

2. Use Your Imagination!

If you see someone treating water in a way that isn't good, it probably won't help to say, "Hey, stop that! You're hurting the water." Instead you might say, "I hope people all around the world aren't doing _____. Because that water is going to become our drinking water!" You can explain that water travels in a big cycle. It really will come back to you!

Or you might decide to say:

_____

3. Learn While You Listen!

Be sure to say why you care about water. But don't be the only one who does the talking. Ask the other person what she knows about water and keeping it clean. Help get her on the right track!

Here's something important I learned about water by talking with other people:

I'll be kind when I tell _____ to _____ by _____ .

A Cool, Watery Treat!

Brownie WOWs can make you thirsty! Ask an adult to help you prepare this colorful drink to celebrate your WOW journey.

Watermelon Cooler

• 2 cups watermelon chunks (with seeds removed)

• 1 cup cracked ice or ice chips

• ½ cup plain yogurt (nondairy yogurt works too)

• ½ tablespoon honey

• a pinch of ginger

• a few drops of vanilla extract

Put all ingredients in a blender. Blend until smooth.

This makes enough for you and two friends.

Cool math: If you and five Brownie friends wanted watermelon coolers, how would you change the recipe so each of you could have one?

Time for a WOW!

Being an Advocate!

An advocate is someone who influences how other people do things—with the goal of doing things better. By inspiring others to Take Action for water, you are influencing people to save and protect a precious resource. That's doing something better! That's being an advocate!

What people can you get to join you in saving and protecting water? How about everyone at school? Neighbors on your block? Who else could help save water?

Saving and Protecting Water

What You and Your Brownie Team Can Do!

Shut Off That Faucet!

Where do you notice running water? When do you and your family let faucets run when you could shut them off?

BE KIND TO WATER!

SAVE: How about making signs to encourage people to turn off the faucet. Yes, they should wash well, but they shouldn't use more water than they need. Suggest they not wash their hands longer than the time it takes to sing "Happy Birthday."

Where could you get permission to post your signs? At home, by the sinks and in the shower? At school? In your town library?

SHARE: How much water is saved by people following your advice? Share what you've done with those in charge of the buildings you've helped. Inspire others to join in.

Stop That Leak!

Where do you notice toilets running or water dripping? Check at home, and at your school and town library—any buildings you can think of!

SAVE: Get others to join you! Who is in charge of the buildings where you found leaks? Whom can you report your "leaky evidence" to so that the leaks get fixed?

SHARE: Think how much water you might save by fixing every leak you find! Share what you've done and get others to spot and fix leaks, too.

Choose a Broom, Not a Hose!

Where do you notice people hosing down driveways and sidewalks? Does your family do that? If you live in a city, maybe you've even seen store owners hosing down the sidewalks on a rainy day!

SAVE: How about getting your neighbors, your school, or businesses in your town to join in? Encourage everyone to stop hosing down sidewalks and driveways and to start sweeping instead. Think of all the water to be saved!

SHARE: Tell those in charge of your town how many people have agreed to put down their hoses. Spread the word and get even more people to join in!

Ban Bottles!

How often do you drink water out of small, store-bought plastic bottles? Do you really need to, or is there another way?

You might not realize it, but it takes 3 gallons of water to make the plastic for every gallon of water that gets bottled. That's a lot of water not being saved!

Maybe you and your family drink bottled water because the tap water in your town doesn't taste good or your family is worried about it not being pure.

Maybe sometimes, such as after a storm, the water from your tap is muddy looking. Talk to those in charge of your town's water supply to find out why the water tastes or looks yucky. Maybe there is a way to make it better. Would a water filter on your tap help?

If not, and you really can't drink your tap water, ask your parents to buy bottled water in large containers only. Have a family member pour what you need into a glass or a container you can carry and use over and over again.

SAVE: Get others to join in! How about asking your school, your sports teams, your neighbors, maybe even your whole community? Ask everyone to stop buying small plastic bottles of water.

SHARE: Let even more people know what you've accomplished. Maybe you can influence store owners in your area to stop selling small bottles of water. Now, that's being an advocate!

Grow Water-Smart Plants!

Where do you see plants that need lots of watering? Look in your home, your backyard, and your neighborhood. How about at school or your place of worship? Check out any nearby parks, too!

SAVE: Who is in charge of the plantings in your community? In your neighborhood park? At your school? What might you ask them to change? Can they replace water-hungry plants with ones that live naturally in your area with little water? Once you ask one or a few people, whom else can you ask?

SHARE: You may not see a change right away, but you can still share your effort and ask even more people to join you! It will make others aware of the water they might be wasting. It will get them thinking about how to save water. That's influencing people and being an advocate! Good for you!

Part 3

Underwater World

Brownie Elf was about to enjoy some tea with her grandmother when Jamila, Campbell, and Alejandra let her know they were ready for another water adventure.

So Brownie Elf and Grandmother Elf packed up their tea and sweets and, with a *poof*, got themselves to the pier. A strange object bobbed in the water nearby. "Over here," the elf called out to the girls.

"What is that?" asked Alejandra.

"A submarine, maybe," said Jamila.

"Looks like a spaceship to me," said Campbell.

"Good thinking, both of you," said Grandmother Elf. "It's a small ship used for deep-sea exploring. It's called a submersible—sub for short. Oh, and I'm Brownie Elf's grandmother from Scotland. I've brought homemade snacks for our voyage." She showed them her basket with yummy-looking sandwiches and cookies, which she called biscuits. She also carried a big jug of tea.

"Hello" and "Thank you," the girls said.

"Ready to come aboard?" Brownie Elf asked.

"Maybe we'll see sunken treasure," said Jamila.

"Or a dolphin!" Alejandra added.

"Let's get going. There's lots to see," Brownie Elf said. "Who wants to drive this sub first?"

The girls looked at one another with wide eyes.

"It's not hard to learn," said Brownie Elf as she opened the hatch and helped her grandmother in. "I'll show you every step along the way!"

"May I go first?" asked Campbell.

"Certainly," said the elf. "Everyone, hop aboard."

Jamila and Alejandra strapped themselves in, each beside a porthole.

Subs are more than sandwiches

Imagine five 2,000-pound elephants standing on top of Brownie Elf's sub. That's how much weight, from water and the air above, pushes against a sub when it is in the deep sea. To stay safe, ocean explorers have to be inside a special cabin that won't collapse from all that pressure. That's why subs were invented—to allow people to explore deep in the sea.

The long shape of Navy subs gave submarine sandwiches their name. But submersibles for deep-sea exploring come in lots of shapes and sizes.

Marine biologists help engineers design these underwater ships. And they always name them. *Alvin*, the most famous submersible, is almost 50 years old. It's been on 4,200 dives! Below is what *Alvin* looks like.

If you and your Brownie friends enjoy dreaming up subs, ask some adults to help you make models of them. You could even make them out of materials that need to be recycled, like plastic bottles, cardboard, and paper.

Henry Groskinsky/Time & Life Pictures/Getty Images

Campbell sat in the pilot's seat, slipped into her seatbelt, and waited for her instructions. Brownie Elf and her grandmother sat on either side of her.

"OK, push the ON button," Brownie Elf said.

The sub gurgled and roared. Bubbles floated around. "First level, first button, right?" Campbell asked.

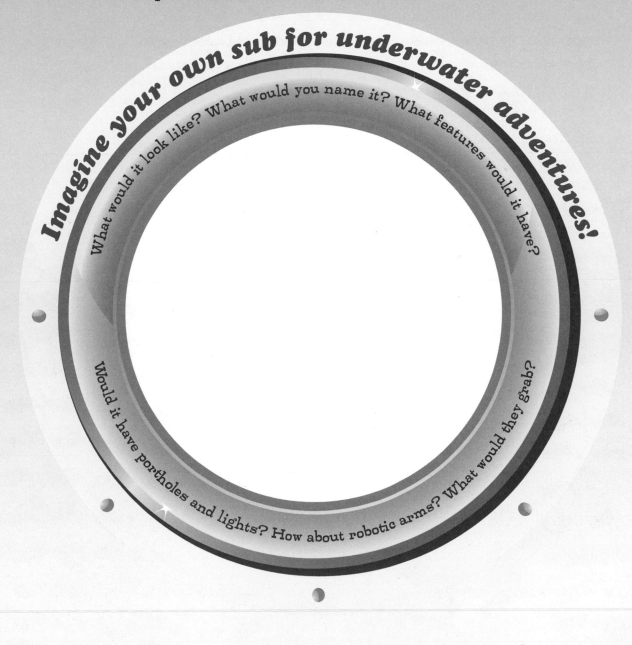

Imagine your own sub for underwater adventures! What would it look like? What would you name it? What features would it have? Would it have portholes and lights? How about robotic arms? What would they grab?

"That's right, the Sunlight Zone," the elf said. Down the sub went, passing huge plants that, together, looked like waving forests. Tiny shrimp swarmed the plants' leaves. A harbor seal swam by and then a purple-striped jellyfish. Hundreds of little anchovies raced past, a whole school.

"Those plants look like big trees," said Jamila.

"That's kelp, a very big kind of seaweed," said Grandmother Elf. "All kinds of things get made from seaweed—even ice cream has seaweed in it!"

Seaweed, also known as saltwater-dwelling algae, comes in many varieties. Have you seen
NORI in sushi?
HIJIKI as a vegetable or salad?
TOSAKA as salad?
WAKAME in soups and salads?
KONBU in soup?

"Now," she said, "let's find a coral reef. My wee home in Scotland is surrounded by water, but it's too chilly for coral to live there."

Brownie Elf smiled. "We'll see a coral reef soon. Campbell, push the SLOW button as we get closer—we don't want to disturb the coral. Lots of coral together form reefs. The reefs are home to a lot of sea life. And those reefs help people, too. They make useful things like medicines."

Campbell slowed the sub just as a bright, new underwater world popped into view.

Water Wisdom

One hot afternoon you go outside and notice everything looks wilted and droopy. What should you do?

A. Get the hose and soak every blade of grass. Don't stop until there are puddles everywhere.

B. Race to tell everyone, "You need to water right now."

C. Tell your parents the lawn needs help, but mention it's better not to water until the sun goes down.

Answer: C—When it's hot, water evaporates—as much as 3 gallons out of every 10 can be lost. Also think about changing some of your grass to plants that don't need a lot of water. You can learn about low-water plants from gardeners and plant stores in your community. What good WOW approach can you use to ask your parents about this?

"The reef is so beautiful," said Alejandra, taking out her notebook. "I'm going to sketch it. Then I can make a painting of it when I get home."

"Look at the colors!" said Jamila. "Even more than in a rainbow."

"It's like a giant aquarium. So many creatures! We can't possibly count them all," Campbell said.

Grandmother Elf pointed out spiny sea urchins, ink-squirting cuttlefish, jellyfish lit up like neon signs, bright blue Christmas tree worms, and a white-topped coral crab. There were big whale sharks, too, and giant manta rays.

"Hey, there's a dolphin," said Alejandra. "I got my wish!"

"So many different creatures live in this one sea community," Grandmother Elf explained. "That's why it's important to keep the ocean clean. A clean ocean keeps coral healthy. If coral isn't healthy, plants and fish can't live in it."

The girls nodded and spent a long time looking at the awesome underwater sights.

Finally, Grandmother Elf spoke again. "Do you know we've been watching silently for an hour?" she asked. "That's a lovely thing to do, isn't it—just taking in the wonders of the world? That's the best way to love nature."

OCEAN LOVER

Katherine Fondacaro cares about fish, sea turtles, and other ocean dwellers. Katherine is a Girl Scout who lives in Oceanside, Long Island, in New York. She's 16 years old and a master scuba diver.

Every summer Katherine joins a group of scientists who sail to the British Virgin Islands in the Caribbean. There they study the ocean and the changes they see. Katherine has seen big changes in the coral reefs and fish.

Coral reefs provide shelter and food for fish, but they are also very fragile. In recent years, many reefs have become "sick" because of water pollution. If reefs aren't healthy, the fish living near them can't be healthy, either. Once a coral reef dies, the fish leave the area because they have no home anymore.

"I've noticed the dying coral," Katherine says. "And I can recognize a place and say, 'You know, there was coral here a year ago, and there were fish here. Where did they go?'"

Katherine wants to study marine biology in college and then live and work in the British Virgin Islands so she can continue to study the ocean.

Until then, she wants to teach others about the changes she has seen.

I'm ___8___ years old.

When I'm 16, the year will be 20_2_8_.

When I'm 16, I hope to be an expert at

_____ .

What have you learned about water that you will share with others?

_____

_____

Katherine is 16 and an expert diver!

When I'm 16, I want to be a diver, too!

"An hour already?" Campbell said. "I guess it's time for someone else to drive. Who's next?"

Jamila slid into the pilot's seat. When her finger neared the MIDDLE button, Brownie Elf nodded.

Jamila pushed and the sub gurgled again, going down and down, much deeper than scuba divers go. The light outside the sub changed from soft green to almost gray, like twilight.

"Better turn on the headlights," Brownie Elf said. "That's why this part of the sea is called the Twilight Zone."

Water Wisdom

Your older brother takes the longest showers on Earth. What do you think about it?

A. There should be a rule against bathroom hogs.

B. You want to be his age so you can take long showers, too.

C. He needs to get smarter about using water.

Answer: C—Cutting a shower by one minute can save 800 gallons of water a year. If everyone in the United States cut showers by a minute, we'd save 160 billion gallons a year. That's enough to fill 2.6 trillion glasses of water! So, now that you know the answer, how will you tell your brother in a good way?

"Whoa!"
said Jamila as
the lights came on.
"Look at that jellyfish with
polka dots. You can see right through it!
And are those mountains?"
"They're called seamounts," Brownie Elf explained.
"Thousands of years ago they were volcanoes. Now only the
tops of them can be seen. They're like mountains in the sea."
As the sub plunged farther down, past twilight into the
dark, what looked like a large building glided by.
"Wow! What's that?" the girls shouted.

MAKING PET PETS

Have you ever thought of making a pet from a PET? Turn over a plastic drink bottle and you will often see the number 1 and the letters "PET." PET stands for polyethylene terephthalate, a kind of plastic that's very strong and lasts a long, long time.

Guess what artist **Miwa Koizumi** does with plastic water bottles? Instead of recycling them in a bin, she makes them into sea creatures. With scissors and tools, she carves the bottles into wiggly jellyfish, anemones, coral, and even sea slugs.

Miwa collects empty containers on the street to make into pets. She sees them as "small creatures." "Everywhere I go, they are waiting for me," she says.

Miwa grew up in Japan and now lives in Brooklyn, New York. Some of her jellyfish have long, red tentacles; others are blue or green. The good news is none of them will ever sting you!

What other sea creatures would you like to see Miwa make from a PET?

"Just a whale going down for dinner," Brownie Elf said with a laugh. "Let's follow."

Jamila steered the sub carefully, following the whale's powerful tail as the animal went deeper and deeper before it leveled off.

"How far down are we?" asked Alejandra.

"More than half a mile," said Brownie Elf. "This is where some whales come to feed. It's the Midnight Zone." Watching the whale feed gave Grandmother Elf an idea. "Are you girls hungry, too?" she asked, opening her picnic basket.

While they were enjoying their sandwiches and biscuits and tea, the girls felt the sub shake a little. Then they heard a loud boom. The whale turned with a start and glided away.

"It's so huge, but the noise seemed to scare it," said Campbell. "That's too bad."

Bringing the World Together with Tea!

Tea is a popular drink in Scotland, Grandma Elf's homeland. It's popular in other countries, too, like China and India.

Juliette "Daisy" Gordon Low, the founder of Girl Scouts, liked to drink tea. Her camping house even had a tea room.

Daisy traveled to India in 1908 and to Scotland in 1911. It's likely she enjoyed tea in both those countries. While in Scotland, Daisy ate hot buttered scones and bread with butter and strawberry jam—all of which go perfectly with tea!

In 1911, Daisy also visited England, another country where tea is popular. That was just a year before she started the Girl Scouts. While in England, Daisy hosted a tea for 60

"It isn't just pollution from runoff and trash that can hurt sea life," said Grandmother Elf. "Sometimes noise is pollution, too. In water, noises sound louder than on land, and they carry farther. Deep-sea creatures can be disturbed by them."

"How much deeper does the ocean get?" asked Alejandra.

"The deepest parts of the ocean floor are more than five miles down—too far for this short trip," said Brownie Elf. "Ali, why don't you drive now?"

As Alejandra moved the sub deeper, the ocean looked darker. A light flashed up ahead, and then to the side, and then another, like silent fireworks.

"Do you think there are other explorers down here?" asked Campbell. "Are those headlights?"

members of the Girl Guides.

A tea party is a nice way to bring people together. Daisy brought a lot of people together when she started the Girl Scouts and changed the world for girls. When you want to make the world better, refreshments always help!

What can your Brownie team do to bring people together to protect Earth's water?

"No," said Brownie Elf. "Those are sea creatures that give off light. It's the only light in this complete darkness. Many deep-sea creatures can make their own light from chemicals in their bodies."

"Like fireflies in the summer?" said Campbell.

"Exactly," said Brownie Elf. "Look ahead."

In a beam from the sub's headlights, the girls could see the strangest creatures yet. Sea worms and huge eels floated by, as did a fish with a flashing light on top of its head. There were fish with long tails, and see-through creatures that looked like they were made of glass.

"There's a red light over there," said Campbell. "Another fish," said Brownie Elf. "These creatures tend to stay in one place, flashing their lights to attract mates or food. The one with the lamp on his head is an angler fish."

The girls sat quietly, amazed. Finally Alejandra asked, "Is it cold out there?"

"Close to freezing," said Brownie Elf. "But other places in the sea have warm water spurting up, so the water is almost hot there."

"What an awesome world down here," said Jamila. "I'd like to stay longer and see it all."

"Maybe you'll invent a sub of your own someday," said Campbell.

As the sub began to slowly rise toward home, Campbell said, "Just because people don't know about the life below, they think it's OK to throw stuff in the ocean. We should tell everyone about life in the deep sea."

"Maybe I could make lots of paintings to show," said Alejandra.

"Good idea, Ali," said Jamila. "Maybe I'll learn more about subs and how they work."

The girls agreed to work together to decide the best way to tell everyone about the wonders of the sea. Grandmother Elf said she liked that idea. It showed they were thinking as a team.

Before they knew it, the sub was at the surface. Brownie Elf popped the hatch. "After you," the girls said to Grandmother Elf before stepping out.

"Now it's your turn to tell others what you saw," Brownie Elf told the girls.

"We will," the girls said as they waved good-bye. Grandmother Elf and Brownie Elf waved back. And then, with two *poofs,* they disappeared.

Water Wisdom

How much water should you use while brushing your teeth?

A. Keep the faucet off until it's time to rinse.

B. Leave the faucet on the whole time.

C. Keep an egg timer in the bathroom. Use it to tell you when brushing time is over. Once you've finished brushing and rinsing, you can turn the faucet off.

Answer: A—If you turn the faucet off while brushing your teeth, you can save several gallons of water every day.

Time for a WOW!

Good Friends Keep Their Promises

Brownie Elf was about to enjoy some tea with her grandmother when the girls called on her. She had promised them a water adventure and she had felt their excitement. So she convinced Grandmother Elf to pack up the tea and join her on an adventure.

> Keeping your promises is one of the best ways to WOW people and show you care.

When you keep a promise, what line of the Girl Scout Law are you living?

_____

When have you given up something fun to keep a promise or help a friend?

_____

Coral Reefs

Coral reefs are found in warm ocean waters. They provide food and shelter for thousands of fish and sea animals—they're like bustling cities under the sea!

Two hundred kinds of birds, 30 kinds of whales, dolphins, and porpoises, 1,500 kinds of fish, and 400 kinds of coral live on the 1,600-mile-long Great Barrier Reef in Australia. The largest coral reef in North America is the Florida Reef Tract. It is the third-largest coral reef in the world.

Climate change, pollution, and too much fishing hurt coral reefs. Some of the world's coral reefs have already disappeared. One-third of the remaining coral reefs are in danger of disappearing.

Scientists think that someday they might find a cure for cancer in the sea life of coral reefs. That won't be possible if the reefs disappear.

Coral reefs might look like plants, but they're actually hard structures created by tiny animals called corals. When corals die, their skeletons form reefs.

Worlds of (Under) Water

The Brownie friends saw many worlds beneath the ocean's surface. Scientists who study the deep sea divide it into these regions:

Ocean Surface
Sunlight Zone, where some light gets in
Twilight Zone, where it feels like dusk
Midnight Zone, where there is no light

Match these creatures and features to the regions the girls explored.
Remember: Some creatures can swim in more than one zone.

Anglerfish
Harbor seal
Kelp

Whale
Coral
Seamount

Answers: Coral and kelp live almost exclusively in the Sunlight Zone; whales and harbor seals are mammals that can be found on the surface and also swimming in the Sunlight Zone; anglerfish are in the Twilight Zone; they are also in the Midnight Zone, where it's cold and pitch-black. Seamounts are found there, too.

Ocean
Surface

Sunlight
Zone

Twilight
Zone

Midnight
Zone

The Wonder of Whales

Whales are the world's biggest animals. The blue whale can weigh up to 300,000 pounds. That's bigger than the biggest dinosaur.

The blue whale eats the tiniest fish, so it eats a lot of them. Each day it eats 40 million tiny fish! In just one mouthful, a blue whale can eat and drink 15,000 gallons of food and water.

DEEP SEA EXPLORER

Edith "Edie" Widder loves learning about sea creatures that give off light. She is a biologist, a deep-sea explorer, and an inventor, too. She spends a lot of time studying the ocean dwellers that flash in the dark.

Years ago, when Edie was an 11-year-old at Girl Scout camp in New Hampshire, her mom sent her maps that showed the faraway places her family would visit when camp ended.

Time for a WOW!

Teaming and Planning to Save Water

When Edie Widder had trouble seeing certain creatures deep in the ocean, she didn't give up. She thought about what she needed. She got help from others and also invented a gadget. Then she educated and inspired others by starting the Ocean Research and Conservation Association, or ORCA.

Her way of working was definitely a WOW! How about you? Try following Edie's example to work toward your Save Water and Share Water awards.

Soon Edie was swimming around the coral reefs of Fiji, a group of islands in the South Pacific.

"The reefs in Fiji hooked me on marine sciences," Edie says.

Later she decided to focus on deep-sea creatures that give off light. But she ran into a problem: The bright lights of her equipment scared the creatures away. So Edie worked with engineers to invent a special system called Eye in the Sea, or EITS for short. EITS is a special camera that senses light and can film these sea creatures without disturbing them. Using EITS, Edie filmed rare sharks and jellyfishes in their natural habitats and discovered a new kind of large squid.

Engineers invent things! What might you like to invent someday?

_____

_____

_____

_____

Here are the steps to follow:

My Brownie team and I want to_____

_____

We're going to get help from _____

And then together we will _____

Then we are going to inspire others by talking with them about

_____

and maybe even asking them to _____

A FLOATING DUMP

The world's largest dump is in the far Pacific Ocean. This trash island is so big, it weighs more than 100 million tons! And it has a name: the Great Pacific Garbage Patch.

The patch collects trash from all over the world. But it wasn't planned—the moving water just naturally brings all the trash together.

Most of the garbage in the patch is made of plastic, which is dangerous in the ocean. More than 1 million animals die each year by becoming entangled in plastic garbage or eating it (they mistake it for food).

When **Megan and Renee Handley** of Santa Barbara, California, were Girl Scout Juniors, they let their community know about the dump. "Do not dump anything into the ocean," they warned. "And don't use plastic bags."

Some cities have banned plastic bags. What kind of bags do you use? What is your community doing?

Jay Directo/AFP/Getty Images

Time for a WOW!

Inspiring Others

You and your Brownie team may want to do something to stop plastic from landing in the ocean. Remember those WOW Tips for Talking? Well, here are some more to get you going!

 When you prepare to talk to others about doing good, be sure you and your Brownie team can answer the following questions with nice, clear statements that get people interested:

• The problem we want to solve is _____

• This matters to us because _____

• More people could help us by _____

What else do you think people will want to know?

_____

These are your "top" messages for inspiring others. Practice saying them and be sure to use your own special energy to "deliver" them!

And now that you have your top messages, get creative about how you use them. Can you write a song that will get these messages across? How about making a poster that shows them all? Or you might try creating a commercial like the ones you see on TV. Use your imagination!

LOVE OF WATER

Alexandra Cousteau in India

Alexandra Cousteau has always thought of the water as her home, and no wonder: Her grandfather was the famous underwater explorer Jacques Cousteau. He helped teach her how to swim when she was just 4 months old, and when she was 7 years old, he taught her how to dive. Since then she's been doing a lot of swimming and diving.

To share her love of water, this former Girl Scout created Blue Legacy, a program that teaches people about water and inspires them to do something to save and protect it. She has traveled the world's waters to raise awareness of this precious resource.

"People think that their impact on water is only between the faucet and the drain, and that's simply not true," Alexandra says. Our food takes water to grow, and other things we buy take water to manufacture and to send to stores. Most people don't think about these uses of water.

"People need to understand that their impact on water is great and affects other people around the world," Alexandra says. "We are in the same boat as people in Bangladesh or people in the Congo, or people in Brazil or the Middle East. We live on a water planet and that water is the support system of the life cycle."

Tea, a Drink with Jam and Bread!

Do you know the song "Do-Re-Mi" from the movie *The Sound of Music*? One of its lines is "Tea, a drink with jam and bread!"

You might like to sing the song with your friends and have some special fun with the tea line! Here's a recipe you can try:

Peppermint Ice Tea
Makes four 8-ounce servings.
• Put 2 peppermint tea bags in a pitcher.
• Ask an adult or older friend to add 4 cups of boiling water to the pitcher.
• Let the tea steep for 3 minutes.
• Stir in a teaspoon of honey if you like your tea sweet. A bit of cinnamon tastes good, too.
• Refrigerate. When cool, pour over ice cubes. Colorful straws and fresh mint will make your tea into a festive tea party.

Tea for Sunny Days

To make Peppermint Sun Tea, just use cold water instead of hot. Then place the pitcher in the sun and let the tea brew for no more than 3 hours.

Loving the Great Outdoors!

The Brownie friends are enjoying a lot of outdoor adventures. How about you? Maybe you'll go camping for a night or hiking for a day.

What will you do to be prepared? _____

What will you pack? _____

What water do you hope to see? _____

Part 4

Water Power

"Wow, this is awesome," Campbell said. She was looking around at the fast-running Colorado River. Brownie Elf had brought the girls to the Grand Canyon in Arizona for one more water adventure.

They stood in bright sunlight near the river at the bottom of the enormous canyon. Around them, walls of rock rose toward the sky. The walls seemed as high as skyscrapers. And the rock was so many different colors, stacked like layers of marble cake. Some of the rock was sharp and jagged. Some was smooth. Some layers were deep red. Others were cream-colored or gray.

The girls had never seen such an amazing sight.

"Can you imagine how this canyon was made?" Brownie Elf asked.

"I *know* it has to do with water," Jamila said thoughtfully. "But how could water do something so big and so beautiful?"

WORDS
WORTH
KNOWING

When you build a sand castle on the beach, water can rush in and steal half the castle from you. Wind, water, or ice can do the same thing to even bigger objects—like shorelines and mountains. That's EROSION.

"After a heavy rain, have you seen how water can carve little 'rivers' in the dirt?" Brownie Elf asked. "Or maybe you've built a sand castle on the beach and the next day the waves have torn it down?"

The girls nodded.

"That's waterpower," Brownie Elf said. "When water moves over rock or dirt, it wears it away slowly, over time. That's called **erosion**. The way Earth looks is changing all the time because of water's power."

She pointed to the top of the canyon. "Five million years ago, the river flowed up there. It took all that time to cut away the rocks. Now, look at the canyon walls. The layers of rock look the same on both sides because they were once connected by the same kind of rock."

"Wow! They really do look the same," Campbell said, peering at one wall and then the other.

Alejandra was looking down at the river. "What happened to all the rock that was cut away—the stuff that used to fill this space?" she wondered.

"The river dropped it in new places—to form new land—and then the water ran into the ocean," Brownie Elf explained. "Now, Ali, would you like to see the canyon walls up close?"

"Yes!" Alejandra said.

"Yes!" and "Yes!" the other girls echoed.

"Over here," Brownie Elf called. "I've turned our bubble into an elevator!"

Loving the Great Outdoors

What amazing natural wonders have you seen near or far from home?

_____

What amazing sights do you hope to see someday?

_____

The four entered the bright bubble elevator and the doors closed with a soft *whoosh*.

"Some people take boats or rafts down the river," Brownie Elf said with a smile. "I thought you'd like to travel up the canyon walls. They're so high, an elevator is the best way to travel!"

"May I push the buttons?" Alejandra asked. "How about this one?"

"That's for Redwall," Brownie Elf said. "That's the name of one rock layer."

Campbell pointed to another button.

"And this one?"

"Devonian. Purple rock," the elf replied.

"Purple is my favorite color," Jamila said. "Let's go there."

Water Wisdom

Your dentist taught you how to floss your teeth. What should you do with the floss once you've used it?

A. Put it in the garbage.

B. Wash it down the drain.

C. Throw it in the toilet.

Answer: A—Things that get flushed down the toilet can end up in rivers and streams, where they can hurt fish and other wildlife. Dental floss can clog drains, so it is best thrown in the garbage. It is not a good idea to reuse floss, because it will have bacteria on it.

Alejandra pressed the button. The Devonian layer was narrow and sparkled in the sunlight. Way below the four friends, the silvery belt of the Colorado River twisted through the canyon.

"Let's go higher," Jamila said. She picked the button for Hermit shale.

The four climbed through dark pink and light red rock. They stopped close to the top of the canyon. They were silent as they looked out, down, and around. The canyon was so huge.

"Look, there's something moving there," Alejandra called. Among the shrubs, they saw the flash of a bushy tail. "I think it's a squirrel."

"Since we're on the canyon's south rim, you saw a white-bellied Abert's squirrel," said Brownie Elf. "On the north rim, you'd see a black-bellied Kaibab squirrel."

"Why are there two kinds of squirrels here?" Alejandra asked.

"Before there was a canyon, there was only one kind of squirrel," Brownie Elf explained. "When the canyon separated into two sides, the squirrels were separated, too. Over the years, they adapted to the different environments on each side and started to look different."

Campbell pushed another button. Suddenly, the girls and Brownie Elf gazed down at a gigantic concrete structure rising above the river.

"Does this remind you of the beaver dam in the wetlands?" Brownie Elf asked.

The three girls laughed and shook their heads.

"It might not look the same, but it's a dam. All dams do one thing: hold back water," Brownie Elf said. "When people build dams they often use the water to make electricity."

"How?" Alejandra asked.

"When water flows downhill, its energy can be used to turn machines called turbines. When the turbines turn, they make electricity that can be sent to people's homes," the elf said.

A falcon flew by so close they could see its pale chest feathers.

"But when people build a big dam," Brownie Elf continued, this time in a quieter voice, "it can be hard for some animals. A dam can make it hard for fish to swim up the river to lay their eggs or to swim downstream to the ocean. Sometimes, when really big dams are built, wetlands near rivers disappear. That means no more home for the animals that lived there and depended on wetlands plants for food. We have to find ways to protect the animals and help people."

"Can we help?" Campbell asked.

"You can," said Brownie Elf. "Just try every day to do one thing to save water. When you use less water and less electricity, that helps people and animals.

"Another way to help is to tell others what you know," Brownie Elf continued.

The Hoover Dam

Las Vegas gets 90 percent of its water from Lake Mead.

The Hoover Dam is on the Colorado River, 30 miles from Las Vegas. It was built in 1935. It is 726 feet high and 1,244 feet long. The river, which flows in and out of Lake Mead, is more than 1,400 miles long. It flows southwest from Colorado through Utah, Arizona, Nevada, California, and Mexico.

Lake Mead was created when the Hoover Dam blocked the Colorado River and flooded the Mojave Desert. Lake Mead, the largest U.S. manmade lake, supplies water to 22 million people across the Southwest.

The Hoover Dam generates about 4 billion kilowatt-hours of hydroelectric power each year for use in Arizona, Nevada, and California.

"Not just the big things that you learned about water but smaller things, too. Small things—and small acts—can be very important. A lot of small, positive acts can add up to very big, positive changes for water."

"I think I know what you mean," said Campbell. "Yesterday I asked my sister to turn off the water when she brushes her teeth. But first I held a bowl under the faucet while it ran and showed her how much water she was wasting. Does that count?"

Water Wisdom

It's your job to give your cat fresh water every day. If there's water left before you refill the bowl, what should you do with it?

A. Pour it down the drain.

B. Water the houseplants with it.

C. Pour it into the trash.

Answer: B—Try to reuse and save water in every way you can. Remember: Every drop you save makes a difference.

"And I asked my father to fix our leaky faucet," Jamila said. "I put a bucket under it overnight to show him how much water it was wasting."

"And I never use a hose anymore to clean the driveway," Alejandra added. "I sweep. I saw how much water was just running into the street."

Brownie Elf smiled. "Yes, those are all small but important things. My job is complete! You really love water and care about saving it and keeping it pure so there is enough for the world to share. Every day you will learn more and teach others, too."

And so, the four friends said good-bye. "We'll always remember what you taught us," the girls said. "We'll pass it on all our lives."

Mottoes and Secret Words!

Today the Girl Scout motto is "Be Prepared."

In earlier days, the Brownie motto was "Lend a Hand." It was abbreviated to a secret word: LAH.

Back in 1945, Brownies had several mottoes (and secret words!) to choose from:

- Do Your Best (DYB)
- Help Other People (HOP)
- Think of Others (TOO)
- Go Ahead (GA)

Adults were told that mottoes and secret words "are important only when the girls themselves originate them and think they are important."

Think up your own motto and secret word!

_____

_____

Why are they important to you?

_____

_____

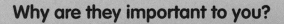

Time for a WOW!

Share What You Know and Get Others to Join in, Too!

Remember when Jamila, Campbell, and Alejandra learned all about life in the deep sea? They wanted to teach others about the importance of treating water well. They were so excited that they were all talking at once.

The girls were lost in their own thoughts and ideas.
But they knew they needed to listen to one another.

Before they knew it, an hour had passed! The girls had
listened carefully,
agreed on a shared goal, and
changed their ideas a little to match their goal.

Here's what the girls decided: They would start their big plan to educate and inspire others with a celebration called Wonders of the Deep.

Let's have an art show!

Let's invite an explorer to talk about the deep sea!

Let's tell people about coral reefs!

Campbell would invite a marine biologist to speak and then answer questions.

Alejandra would organize an art show.

Jamila would put together a presentation on coral reefs.

The girls wanted to be sure that Wonders of the Deep really got people to care about water and use it wisely every day. So they brainstormed again.

Imagine that you were brainstorming with them. Suggest two ways the girls can be sure that people learn good and lasting water habits at their event:

_____

The girls want people to do something specific for water, so that their good habits last. What would you ask people to do for water?

_____

Get some friends together and try your own brainstorm! Figure out what you will do to get people involved and keep them involved. What you and your team decide and do will lead to your Save Water and Share Water awards!

BEACH EROSION AND THE BENEFITS OF SEA GRASS

People like to live near the beach or vacation at the beach, and many others depend on the ocean and the beach to earn a living.

Beaches are also important to the animals that live on them and near them, including crabs, shrimp, and many types of birds.

Yet every day, ocean waves come to shore and take away more and more sand from the world's beaches. This process is the same one that cut the Grand Canyon over millions of years.

The roots in hardy plants like sea grasses help hold beach sand in place when waves roar in and the wind blows hard. But as more and more houses are built on the sand (because people like living by the beach!), there are fewer plants to secure the shore. So around the world, beaches are disappearing. On many beaches each year, volunteers plant hundreds of shoots of baby sea grass. They hope their efforts

will prevent erosion. Over time, these new sea grass gardens will help beaches stay stable and maybe even grow larger.

Along the Chesapeake Bay in Maryland and Delaware, Girl Scouts have seen sea grass destroyed by storms and runoff.

Regina Santangelo was 12 in 2006 when she and her Girl Scout friends planted more than 100 bundles of sea grass along the Chesapeake Bay, an hour from her home in Middletown, Delaware. "It was cold and rainy when we each got our bundles of sea grass," Regina recalls. "We did it to prevent erosion because sea grass helps hold the sand together."

The girls made holes in the sand with sticks and planted the grasses as part of a statewide project. One beach resident came out and thanked the girls for their work.

Tides and Wave "Snakes": Moving Water Wonders

One force that makes water move is called a tide. Because of tides, ocean waves sometimes come up high on the shore and sometimes they stay farther out. Tides can also produce a swirling body of water called a whirlpool.

When you drain a bathtub, you can see a very small whirlpool. You can also create a little whirlpool by stirring a spoon in a half-filled glass of water.

Whirlpools also form at the bottoms of waterfalls. Waterfalls form when a stream or a river runs over a rock formation that has a sudden drop and the water rushes downward.

Wind and water together also make waves. Machines can now capture the energy that waves make in the ocean and use it to produce electricity.

Wave energy is captured by long, steel tubes that look like sea snakes. When waves travel through the tubes, they move up and down and side to side—just like a snake. A wave farm in Portugal can produce enough electricity for 1,500 households.

In the future, waves may provide much of the world's electricity.

FLOATING POOLS

Meta Brunzema loves to swim. She is also an architect. One of the WOWs she enjoys is New York City's Hudson River Park. She wondered if she could build a safe, clean place to swim in that river.

Sixty miles up the river, a singer and musician named Pete Seeger was wondering the same thing. He had seen old photos of people swimming in the river, and he knew that it had been clean and safe then.

Meta and Pete's first floating River Pool opened on the Hudson in Beacon, New York. It is 30 inches deep, with flow-through sides and a net bottom stretched like a trampoline. Bright fiberglass seats surround the pool, which can hold 20 swimmers at a time.

This pool "floats" in the river and responds to the motion of the tides and currents. Fish and plant life are not harmed by the pool. And swimmers don't have to worry about pollution or rocks or broken glass or being swept away by the tides.

Meta and Pete are part of a group of people around the world who plan to remake rivers into places where people can once again swim safely.

Time for a WOW!

Patience and Persistence

Meta Brunzema has been waiting for years to build a floating pool in New York City. Doing anything, especially turning a good idea into action, can take time.

Patience is a quality that can help you wait when you have to. Persistence is what will help you move forward even when the finish line seems too far away to keep going.

Have you ever wanted something to happen and had to wait?

_____

What did you learn about yourself while you waited?

_____

What advice can you give to someone who wants to give up?

_____

Is there something that you keep trying to do but haven't finished yet?

_____

What have you learned each time you try?

_____

What are you trying to learn or do with your Brownie team now?

_____

My WOW! Awards

These pages list each thing you must do to earn your WOW awards. Use them to keep track of all you do!

LOVE Water

Name two things you know and love about water, and make and carry out one personal promise to protect water.

What I Love About Water

I thought about all the things I like to do in and with water.

And I listened to all the things my Brownie friends like to do in water.

Then I picked my two favorite things that I love about water:

1. _____

2. _____

My Water Promise

This is how I'm protecting water:

_____

_____

SAVE Water

Do something with your team to protect water or keep it clean.

My Brownie team had a brainstorm to decide what we would do to protect water or keep it clean.

We talked about _____

and then came to a team decision to _____

_____. We accomplished this by

_____ .

This will be good for Earth's water because _____ .

SHARE Water

Educate others about your water efforts, inspire them to join in, and ask them to commit to a water promise, too.

My team educated and inspired these people:

_____

And they promised to _____ .

WOW! This is your final award! It brings together everything you and your team did for water through WOW ways of working.

We know we made a difference for Earth's water because

_____ .

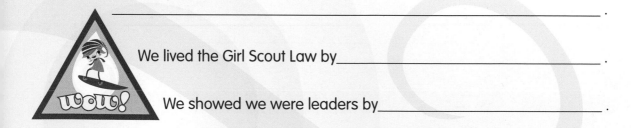

We lived the Girl Scout Law by_____ .

We showed we were leaders by_____ .

What I know about WOW!

With my Brownie team, I've learned that water has three forms: _____ ,

_____ , and _____ .

When water is _____ , I can _____ it

or _____ with it.

When water is a _____ , it usually feels

_____ .

When water is _____ , it could be

_____ or _____ .

What I Want to Do Next to show I love this Blue Planet:

_____ .

Time to Celebrate

Think up a WOW ending to this WOW journey!

How about bringing your very favorite water friends to a WOW tea party?

Do you have a stuffed whale or seal? A water snake or an alligator? How about a cuddly polar bear or penguin? A soaring seagull or big-billed pelican? Bring them along! Give them a cup of tea, too!

If you don't have a water friend, just add flippers to a stuffed bear, or a beaver tail to a bunny. Or make a whole new friend—from recycled paper or a water bottle.

All our water pets (even those made from PET!) help us think about what we love about all the real animals on Earth. They remind us how, as leaders on this Blue Planet, we can show our love for the environment in many ways.

When you gather with your Brownie friends and your stuffed animal friends, choose some special ways to celebrate. You might enjoy:

Introducing your animal friends to one another and letting everyone know why these friends matter.

Thinking about all the different people enjoying different flavors of tea around the world. To make that tea, we all share the world's water!

Thinking about what you will do next.

Thanking all the people you met and who helped you along this journey.

So join a Brownie circle and celebrate. Sing some WOW songs! Maybe even make some rainbows. Keep that water cycle going around and around in one big WOW!

What a Treat! WOW!

Here's a festive watery treat you could make and share at your WOW awards celebration.

Colorful Melon "Cookies"

Get out your favorite cookie cutters. Start with some seedless watermelon or cantaloupe or honeydew melon. Then ask for some help cutting the fruit into slices about one-half inch thick. Cut the colorful fruit with your cookie cutters. Maybe you can make shapes like stars or moons or even gingerbread people.

"Frost" the shapes with plain yogurt or jam. Decorate with raisins, cherry bits, or other fruit; sprinkle with granola. Enjoy!

WOW!

You've Come So Far!

WOW! You're here already-at the end of your WOW journey. Think of all you've seen and learned and accomplished. There's so much, you may feel that loving and protecting your world's water is a journey that never ends.

Think of all your water drops and how they became a river. And how that river flowed into the ocean. In the days and years to come, you will explore many new water drops. And you and your friends will find many new Ways of Working. That's how the Wonders of Water and all Earth's resources will stay pure and replenished for generations to come.

So keep up your teamwork. And keep on inspiring others.

Look back at all the powerful WOWs you've already accomplished. Which was your favorite? Which would you like to explore more?

From now on, when you drink your last sip of water at bedtime and snuggle in with your water creature, you can sleep tight: You and your Brownie friends have become protectors of the precious water on our Blue Planet, and leaders in all you do.